# THE STITCHERY BOOK
## *Embroidery for Beginners*

*This charming hunt scene was embroidered in the Greek Islands
during the 18th century. It is part of an Ionian valance
in* The Metropolitan Museum of Art. Gift of George D. Pratt.

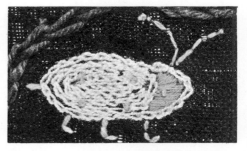

A stitchery bug by Andy.

A stitchery horse
by 12-year-old Karen.

A stitchery doll.

# THE STITCHERY BOOK

## EMBROIDERY FOR BEGINNERS

By Irene Preston Miller and Winifred Lubell

Drawings by Winifred Lubell

DOUBLEDAY & COMPANY, INC.        GARDEN CITY, NEW YORK

*Colorful felt, first stitched,*
*then stuffed, was used for these*
*embroidered hanging birds.*

. . . this book some cunning work doth teach.
(too hard for meane capacities to reach)
So for weake learners, other workes here be,
As plaine and easie as are A.B.C.!
                    *John Taylor, 1640*

When I'm a grown-up woman,
With hair upon my head,
I'll sit and sew till very late
And never go to bed.
          *An Unknown Victorian Girl*

*Part of a charming quilt, appliquéd and embroidered in Brooklyn, N.Y., in 1867. Other sections are shown on page 11.*

## CONTENTS

*East Indian embroidery
with pieces of mica.*
Brooklyn Museum.

*Our thanks . . .*

We want to thank the people who made it possible for us to show you some of the great embroidery treasures in our museums. Our particular thanks go to: Dossah Saulpaugh of the Brooklyn Museum's Design Laboratory; Edith Standen of the Textile Study Room at the Metropolitan Museum of Art; Polaire Weissman of the Metropolitan's Costume Institute; Alice Beer of the Cooper Union Museum; and to the librarians in our village.

We are grateful to Anita Askild and Norman LaLiberté for their banners; to Dorothy Pardon, Gertrude Bush, Lee Cron, Andy Shapiro, Susan Kinyon, and Karen Speller for their stitchery examples, and to Mrs. Ralph Sutton for the use of the delightful quilt made by her grandmother.

We wish to thank the Singer Sewing Machine Company for their assistance.

And our most special thanks go to our two most helpful husbands—Michael Miller for his photography, and Cecil Lubell for his editorial guidance—and to our editor, Carol Drexler, for keeping us on our stitchery path.

Irene Preston Miller
Winifred Lubell
Croton-on-Hudson, N.Y.
1965

*As early as* A.D. *1200 the pre-Incas of Peru made designs like this by stitching feathers to fabric. Drawing is from detail of a large cloak in* The Metropolitan Museum of Art. Dick Fund, 1963.

## STITCHERY IS . . .

. . . simply another word for embroidery. Both terms describe the work of decorating a fabric by the use of a needle and thread.

There are many kinds of stitchery.

Long ago, the Peruvians attached brilliant feathers to their shirts. That was one kind of stitchery. The great Indian chief Powhatan, father of Pocahontas, wore a leather robe "embroidered" with cowrie shells. That was another kind of stitchery. Today, our embroidery work is more often done with traditional threads and yarns, but now too, as in the past, we often decorate our fabrics by stitching onto them such surprising objects as pebbles, driftwood, grasses, leather, beads, or the shining wings of a dragonfly.

All of this comes under the heading of stitchery.

*Drawing of a leather cloak embroidered with shells. It belonged to Powhatan (1550–1618), Indian chief and father of Pocahontas.* Ashmolean Museum, England.

9

It is an ancient craft and has always been considered a very special one. If you had lived in Peru two thousand years ago, and had been one of those picked to spend all her time spinning and dyeing thread, weaving it into cloth, and then decorating it with embroidery, you would have been called a Chosen Woman.

Your great-grandmother was taught to embroider when she was a girl. In those days, this usually meant working with the tiniest of fine stitches. This could be very tedious and perhaps that is why so many girls gave up learning how to embroider.

In this book, the embroidery we will teach you is more inventive and more interesting. In using this book, it will help you greatly if you start at the beginning and move along with us, one step at a time. We urge you not to skip around, though we know you will be tempted to do so. But there is a point to the way we have planned the projects in each chapter, and, if you follow them in order, the experience you gain will help you later when you come to work out your own ideas.

We have enjoyed every minute of the many months it took to make this book. We enjoyed stitching by the fire in the wintertime, while the kitten stole the small balls of brightly colored wool and hid them under the couch. We loved stitching out of doors under the shade trees when summer came. And perhaps most of all, we are grateful for the opportunity of having seen the many stitchery treasures in our great museums.

As you look at the pictures in this book we hope you will sense the pleasure other people took in doing embroidery. And we hope everyone, from nine to ninety, will discover the witchery of stitchery. We wish we could be there to see the results.

*Life in Brooklyn, N.Y., in the 1860s is delightfully revealed in these four details from this old storybook quilt. The four scenes show: (1) two men in a Brooklyn orchard; (2) a miller, in the doorway of his windmill, selling grain to a man on horseback; (3) the dry-goods man with his traveling wagon-store; (4) a street scene with a washerwoman and a hurdy-gurdy man. The whole quilt is beautifully appliquéd and embroidered and shows an imaginative use of striped fabrics and patterned calicoes which must have been lovingly collected for years by the talented Brooklyn woman who made this charming quilt in 1867.*

*This boldly designed head with its enormous earrings was made by a Peruvian embroiderer perhaps 1000 years ago. Detail of fragment in The Metropolitan Museum of Art. Gift of George D. Pratt.*

## Chapter One

## OTHERS WHO HAVE STITCHED

Embroidery is as old as the needle, and the needle is as old as man's earliest civilizations. Needles of bone and bronze have been found in the ancient tombs of Egypt, dating from at least 5000 B.C. We know that the Egyptians wore robes of beautifully embroidered linen and that when Cleopatra, the Queen of Egypt, journeyed down the Nile, the great square sail of her ship was richly decorated with stitchery in royal purple.

On the American continent, the great Paracas weavers and embroiderers of Peru were making some of the world's most magnificent fabrics before the birth of Christ. Embroidery was looked upon as a high form of art. The Peruvians spun their yarns from the luxurious fleece of the llama, the alpaca, and the vicuña, which grazed on the high plateaus of the Andes. These fabrics have been preserved in tombs for more than a thousand years, so that today we can see them in many of our museums. They show the things that were important to the lives of these early Americans—dancers and head-hunters, birds, fish, and four-footed animals.

*Tiny, meticulous flat stitches in silk on satin from Chinese mandarin's coat. Fine 18th-century Canton work.* Collection of Mr. and Mrs. J. Aronson.

Historians have told us that embroidery with silk began in China, for a Chinese empress is said to have discovered silk when she accidentally dropped the cocoon of a silk moth into her cup of tea and then saw the thread unreel in the hot water. From then on, the Empress of China was worshiped as the patroness of silk caterpillars and the secret of their silk thread was guarded zealously. In time, soldiers and travelers from Europe carried home news of the wonderful silkworm in China, but it was not until the sixth century A.D. —after two monks had smuggled some cocoons back to Greece—that the manufacture of silk began on the European continent.

In the elegant court life of the Chinese emperors, embroidery was developed to a high art. A man's station in life or his profession was revealed through the elaborately stitched and many-colored symbols embroidered on his silk and satin robes.

*On a ship like this, with richly embroidered sails, Cleopatra sailed to meet Julius Caesar.*

*Drawing of an embroidery detail from an ancient Japanese kimono. Subtle stitchery like this was used to accent the printed designs.*

In ancient Japan, the art of embroidery was also highly developed. Often the fabric was first painted or printed with a design and then embroidery was used to pick out and emphasize certain areas—the tips of a butterfly's wing, the leaves of a tree, or the petals of a flower.

In India, too, embroidery was a rich and ornate craft, for here precious metals and jewels were stitched into the fabric. The tradition continues today in India, but now instead of jewels they use beads and sparkling pieces of mirrorlike mica to create the glittering effect.

*Detail of large and lively 18th-century Indian Chamba embroidery in* The Metropolitan Museum of Art. Rogers Fund, 1959.

14

In Europe, during the Middle Ages, many a dark and gloomy castle had the brightest room of all set aside for embroidery. Here sat the chatelaine, the mistress of the castle, surrounded by her maidens and the "whole paraphernalia of embroidery frames, materials and implements."

What were they embroidering? Pouches to hang from the belts of young knights off to the wars or the hunt . . . heraldic banners for the armies of the Crusaders . . . or a precious love token, like the one made by Elaine—"lily maid of Astolat."

If poodle collars are often elaborately decorated today, it is not a new idea. In the Middle Ages "the dogs wore collars embroidered with pearls and precious stones" and "the horses were resplendent in trappings of velvet and gold."

*This ancient purse, completely embroidered with tiny stitches, belonged to a lady of fashion in Paris over 600 years ago.*

*Drawing of detail from the famous embroidered Bayeux Tapestry. It shows the Norman cavalry charging the British. The whole tapestry is 230 feet long.*

*Another Bayeux detail—a lookout posted in a tree.*

Books were few in the Middle Ages and not many people knew how to read so that pictures were often used to tell of heroic deeds and great events. The ladies frequently turned their needles to the telling of a story—like the one told in the famous Bayeux Tapestry. In spite of its name, it is not a woven tapestry but is embroidered in wool on pieces of heavy linen sewn together. It was made at the end of the eleventh century and it tells the story of the conquest of England by William of Normandy. It is less than two feet high but over two hundred and thirty feet long.

Times change and so did the embroideries. The ladies turned from battle standards and stories to the embroidery of vestments and linens for the church. During the thirteenth and fourteenth centuries England became famous for its ecclesiastical embroideries.

In England, too, by the time of Henry VIII (1491–1547) and his daughter, Queen Elizabeth, embroidery for personal use had come into vogue and it seemed as though everybody was busy stitching designs on her clothing. Elizabeth herself was an expert needlewoman and her successors in the royal House of Stuart decorated their clothing and their hangings with the family emblem of the carnation and the caterpillar.

In Elizabethan and Stuart England people collected embroidery patterns as we collect recipes, and pattern books were as popular as cookbooks are today. In those days many a servant girl kept a kind of embroidery notebook tucked into the pocket of her apron. Her "paper" was a strip of linen and her "pencil" was a needle and thread. With these she made "notes" of any patterns she liked on her mistress's newest gown or her master's best coat.

*Designs of birds, leaves, and insects, like those drawn above and at lower left, were favorites with Elizabethan embroiderers.*

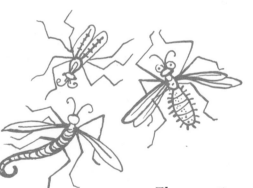

*The carnation and insects on the right were drawn from a 17th-century pattern book for embroiderers called A Schole-House for the Needle.*

*The famous Hungarian shepherd's* szur *coat was elaborately covered with embroidery from collar to hem, and every part of his sweetheart's costume showed her skill in stitchery.*

For the peasants of Europe, embroidery has always been a way of adding color and beauty to their lives—a way open to anyone with a needle and thread. Every country girl was taught to embroider by her mother and they worked together for years on her trousseau, decorating blouses, skirts, petticoats, and pillows.

Young peasant lads were as handsomely outfitted as their sisters in embroidered shirts, coats, and trousers. In Hungary, for example, a *szur* coat was the most cherished possession of a marriageable young man. It was an ankle-length, elaborately embroidered, white wool coat. He hung it over his shoulders and never put his arms into the sleeves, for they were sewn up at the wrists to form convenient pockets for carrying food, money, or tobacco. When he visited his sweetheart, he might—as though by accident—leave his *szur* at her cottage. Next morning, at daybreak, he would stroll by. If it had been hung outside, that would be bad news for the suitor for it meant that he had been rejected. But if the *szur* was still indoors, it was a sign he might ask for the girl's hand in marriage.

*Embroidery detail from a* szur *coat in the Costume Institute of* The Metropolitan Museum of Art. Donor: J. L. Hudson Co., Detroit.

*Gay, brightly stitched designs like these covered the child-bed curtains made in many parts of Europe. These come from Czechoslovakia, as do the designs on our end pages. Source: Textile Folk Art by A. Vaclavik and J. Orel, Spring Books, London.*

Long ago, bed curtains were necessary to provide warmth and protection in unheated houses. They were often elaborately embroidered. In Czechoslovakia, when a baby was born, specially stitched curtains were placed around the baby's cradle and the new mother's bed. The gay designs on these childbed curtains expressed the best wishes of all for the new baby. If it was a boy-child, they usually embroidered a deer, as if to say: "May your little boy grow big and strong and carry himself like a stag." For a girl-child they embroidered blossoms, as if to say: "May your little daughter grow like an apple tree." These curtains hung around the bed during the first six weeks of the baby's life. Then there was a gay party and the baby's god-mother took down the curtains and threw them over the new baby's father, laughingly expressing the hope that they soon might be needed again.

*An Iroquois Indian leather pouch (ca. 1750) with the traditional thunderbird design embroidered in porcupine quills.* Harvard University, Peabody Museum.

*Ermine-trimmed embroidered pouch. Eastern Woodlands Indians.* Courtesy of The Brooklyn Museum.

In our own country, embroidery was an ancient Indian craft. When the English explorers first landed on our shores they found Indian chiefs wearing leather robes embroidered with shells. There were many other kinds of embroidery too. The hair of the buffalo and the moose was dyed and used for stitching designs on clothing, pouches, moccasins, belts, and blankets. The dyed and softened quills of the porcupine were also used for stitchery on leather and birchbark.

Later, when the white settlers came, they traded beads and silk threads with the Indians. The beautiful quill embroidery was replaced with elaborate beadwork and other types of stitchery. Many Indian girls were trained by nuns in convents, and you can see the difference in styles by comparing the silk- and ermine-trimmed bag with the earlier Iroquois leather pouch.

*Detail from a sampler worked in cross stitches by Elizabeth Rowe Terry in 1828. She clothed Adam and Eve and gave them two pet dogs.* Courtesy of The Cooper Union Museum, New York.

During the early days of our country, a girl was expected to sew a fine seam and to know how to embroider by the time she was ten years old. She was taught by her mother how to spin yarn from sheep's wool and strong linen thread from home-grown flax, and she knew how to make colorful dyes from flowers and plants.

Every New England girl learned her embroidery stitches either at home or at school. To show her skill, she made a sampler, sometimes getting her ideas from a pattern book and sometimes inventing designs of her own. Some samplers combined many different stitches. Others used only one stitch. The stitches were designed to show as much as possible of the yarn on the face of the cloth, for in those days thread was far too precious to waste on the back where it wasn't seen. Fabrics were also scarce and the women found ingenious ways to use pieces from worn-out dresses and coats. They were turned into beautiful patchwork and appliqué quilts. Often, on top of the patchwork and the appliqué, they embroidered imaginative designs, as you can see in the picture of the quilt on page 11.

So you can see that at all times and in all places, the ancient craft of stitchery has brought beauty and pleasure into people's lives. It can do the same for you!

*Drawing of detail from a sampler by Abigail Adams in 1789.* Courtesy of The Cooper Union Museum.

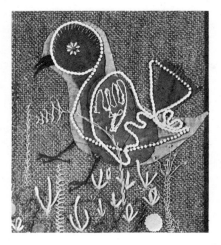

*Detail of a wall hanging
in felt, leather, and embroidery.
The bird is outlined with a
Couched-down string of covered
lead weights. The beak is leather;
the eye—an antique button.*

## Chapter Two

## YOU BECOME A COLLECTOR

Every stitcher is a collector. You will become a hoarder
of bits and scraps that other people throw away. What
a pleasure it is to hunt through your collection and
find just the right background, just the right snip of
purple cloth or orange yarn to fit a special place in
your stitchery.

### THE FABRICS

Embroidery takes a long time; much love and care
goes into it, so think carefully before choosing a background material. It would be good to start a treasure
chest of remnants in different colors and textures.

Good-size background pieces can be found in remnant
stores, upholstery and fabric shops, and in department
stores, which often have small pieces left over from a
big bolt of cloth. You should look for both loosely
woven as well as tightly woven cloths, for fabrics that
are smooth and others that are rough and nubby.

Linen has been a favorite with stitchers since early
Egyptian times. It holds its shape well, is easy to stitch,
and comes in many different weights. But for some
backgrounds you will want to try heavier-weight cottons like canvas and duck, or wool fabrics like tweeds.
Also good for backgrounds are fabrics like felt and Pellon, which are pressed rather than woven materials.

## THE THREADS

Once you start collecting threads, your sewing basket will grow like weeds in the garden. In the ten-cent store or yarn shop you'll find Pearl cotton balls and cotton skeins of embroidery floss, which has six strands and can be divided. Also important are cotton crochet threads and little spools of silk buttonhole twist. Then there are thin, strong crewel wool yarns, which are made from two threads twisted together (two-ply).

Tapestry and knitting yarns are heavier than crewel yarns, and if you have a knitter in the family be sure to ask her to save you all her leftover yarns. If you know a weaver you are especially lucky, for they have many unusual kinds of threads. Another way to get interesting yarns is to unravel loosely woven fabrics.

Everything comes in handy. Part of the excitement of stitchery today comes from the wide assortment of yarns you can find—everything from heavy ropes to fluffy looped mohair, from metallic threads and bumpy rayons to heavy string from the hardware store.

## THE NEEDLES

Needles will all look alike to you at first. However, they have different names and slightly different shapes because each is made to do a different job.

The needle called *Embroidery* or *Crewel* has a fine point and is good for a tightly woven fabric. The one called *Tapestry* has a blunt point and is better for loosely woven fabrics, such as burlap. A *Chenille* needle is short with a fine point and some find it most comfortable. A giant *Rug* needle (sometimes called a tapestry needle) is necessary for very thick yarns. We don't recommend the long *Darner* needle because it's too clumsy to handle, but you will often be using all the other types in one stitchery, depending on the fabric, the yarn, and the type of stitch you are doing.

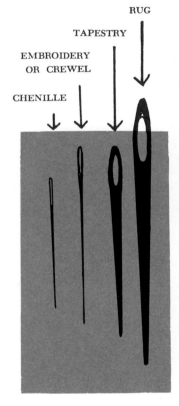

RUG

TAPESTRY

EMBROIDERY OR CREWEL

CHENILLE

*Four types of needles used in embroidery work.*

*Stone needle-pusher found in an ancient Egyptian tomb.*

Take good care of your needles. They are really quite beautiful tools. Store them in a little box and, if they become rusty, rub them lightly on a fine emery board. (In the sixteenth century, needles and pins were not so easily bought, and that's where the term "pin money" came from. It was a special, private allowance for buying pins and needles.)

OTHER HELPFUL TOOLS

A loose-leaf notebook is a great help. It is a place to jot down ideas for future stitcheries, and to store pictures cut out of magazines and postcards from museums. It's a place to keep color combinations you like, and perhaps even small samplers of the stitches you've learned from this book.

Scissors? The best and easiest to use for embroidery is one with a long sharp point.

Plain chalk or dressmaker's chalk is usually all you need to transfer a design to fabric. Don't use a pencil. It won't come off and the thread rarely covers it. If you need to be more exact, you can buy *Dressmaker's Carbon* for tracing a design.

Thimbles? In the past they have been made of stone, bone, ivory and wood, leather and iron, bronze, brass, silver and gold, china, glass, and mother-of-pearl. Today they are usually made of plastic or metal. You need at least one for the middle finger.

And now you're ready to begin!

*Bird-shaped scissors are traditional for embroidery work.*

## Chapter Three

## FIRST THINGS FIRST

### *Three ways to thread a needle*

There are different ways to thread a needle, because there are different kinds of threads. The usual way is to moisten and flatten the thread between your lips and then push it through the needle's eye.

This works when the thread has enough stiffness to stay flat but it won't work with a soft woolen yarn. In that case, fold the yarn over the eye of the needle to crease it (1). Then squeeze the yarn tightly near the fold and pull the needle away (2). Next, bring the eye of the needle down over the fold and thread it (3).

Sometimes, with thicker or very uneven yarns, this method won't work either. Try this: lay the yarn flat on your second finger and press the eye of the needle down on it. Then, with the point of a very fine needle, pull the yarn up through the eye of the large needle (4).

The easiest way to knot an embroidery thread is with a simple loop like a small letter "e". Hold it in place, then bring the end around the back and through the loop (5). Pull it into a tight knot near the end.

You are ready to begin. You should have before you a piece of practice material, preferably about eighteen inches long by twelve inches wide. The needle and thread must be the right size to pull easily through this fabric. Knot the end of the thread and always come through the fabric so the knot is on the back.

## THE FLAT STITCHES

In this chapter we will work with the *flat* stitches. They are easy to make and there are many of them. We begin with a run.

### The Running Stitch

Start so that you can work on the fabric from right to left. This first stitch is like a quick running step: – – – – – – – – –
Sometimes it reaches far ahead: — — — — —
Sometimes it has a short, crowded step: ----------
It can have an even pace, like this: — – — – — –
It can have a varied tempo like this: – — — – — —
The Running stitch makes a good outline and is a fine way to fill in color.

*This bird design can be embroidered entirely with simple Flat stitches.*

26

*Detail from an old Russian bedsheet with borders embroidered in red and blue. Notice the fine use of Running stitches. The horses drawn above were taken from another embroidered Russian sheet. Both are in* The Brooklyn Museum collection.

### The Back Stitch

If the Running stitch left too many open spaces for the outline effect you want, try this:

Start the same way, but take just one stitch.

Then—instead of going forward for your second stitch—go backward to meet the previous stitch. The Back stitch makes a nice clean outline. It's very good for signing your name to a stitchery.

Try sewing your initials on the practice cloth, first with the Running stitch, and then with the Back stitch. For different effects, experiment with different threads.

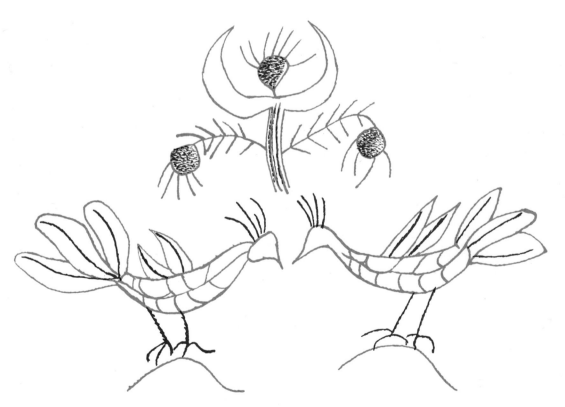

*Designs drawn from an early American sampler (1755)
worked in Back and Stem stitches.* Courtesy of The
Cooper Union Museum, New York.

*Photograph of detail shows the use of Stem stitch in ancient Peruvian cloak.* Metropolitan Museum of Art, gift of George D. Pratt, 1933.

## The Stem Stitch

This is a very old stitch, sometimes called the Outline stitch. This time, start so that you work from left to right. Bring your knotted thread up at the point marked **A.** Go down at **B** and back halfway, coming up at **C.**

The Stem stitch will look best if you try to keep your stitches equal in size. Now go down at **D** and up in the same hole as **B.** Continue in this way, always keeping your thread on the same side. You can use either side but don't switch back and forth.

On your practice piece of material outline a small space with Stem stitch, as you see the birds outlined on the opposite page. Now fill it in, back and forth, with Stem stitch, as the Peruvians always did (see the fish above).

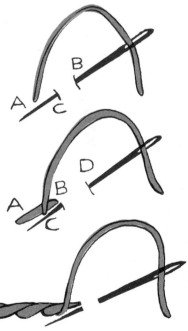

29

*Drawing shows how you can use the Arrowhead and Fern stitches to embroider a flower.*

## NOW TAKE A HOP . . .

Now you know a number of stitches that can be used to make outlines or to get a filled-in, solid effect, but at times you may want to fill a space in a way that will give you a light, airy design. The stitches that follow do this in various ways.

### The Arrowhead Stitch

To begin, come up at **A,** then go down at **B** and up at **C,** then back down in the same hole as **B.** You can line up these little "v's" like birds in flight, or you can scatter them around to fill a space.

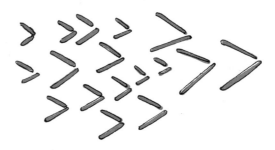

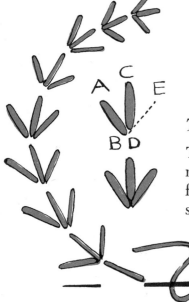

### The Fern Stitch

This is just a little different from the Arrowhead. First make the stitch from **A** to **B.** The second stitch moves from **C** to **D** and is in the center. Then add the third stitch, **E** to **F.** You can see why it's called "Fern."

*Family portrait in Cross stitches with papa holding a giant candlestick. Drawn from an Italian embroidery of 1817 in* The Metropolitan Museum of Art, *bequest of Mrs. Lathrop Harper.*

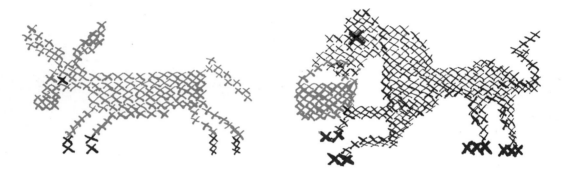

*And two Cross-stitch dogs cavorting in a French sampler of 1800. Brooklyn Museum.*

## The Cross Stitch

This is a very traditional stitch. Years ago, when every little girl made her own sampler, it was often done with nothing but Cross stitches.

Come up at **A.** Go down at **B.**
Come up at **C.** Go down at **D.**
And so on to the next.

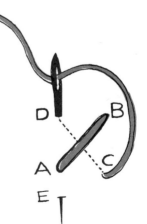

### The Couching Stitch

A quick and interesting way to make large, curving lines or jagged, wiggling lines is with the Couching stitch. You will always Couch when the yarn is thick and irregular and cannot be pulled through the fabric. It is also good for threads which wear out too easily or fray, as does metallic thread.

Choose a few inches of heavy yarn or string and lay it on your fabric. It can be held in place with a pin. Now thread a needle with a different-color yarn, one that can be pulled easily through the material. Near the end, at the right, come up just below but close to the heavy yarn.

Go over the top and back down again.

Couching is useful not only for sewing down thick, heavy yarns but also for a group of thin threads laid down in parallel rows.

The stitch you make on top can move back and forth at a slant or straight across.

### The Thorn Stitch

This is similar to Couching because you lay one thread on top of the fabric and sew it down with Cross stitches. Knot up a short piece of thread and come through. Then knot another thread and make Cross stitches over it to hold it down. It looks like a thorny branch.

*Look carefully and you'll see the delicate
tracery of Herringbone stitches in this handsome
vest from Portugal, in* The Brooklyn Museum collection.

## The Herringbone Stitch

This stitch will surely become one of your favorites.
There are so many ways to make it! By changing the
thickness of the yarn and the size of the stitch, you
can make it look either long and lacy or chunky and
squat.

You sew from left to right. Come up at **A.** Go down at
**B.** Come up at **C,** going back a little way. Go down at
**D.** Go back a little way again and come up at **E.** From
here on, each new line is parallel with the one before
it—**E–F** parallel to **A–B; G–H** to **C–D.**

With a little practice, this stitch moves with a nice
rhythm. In dressmaking it's called the Catch stitch.

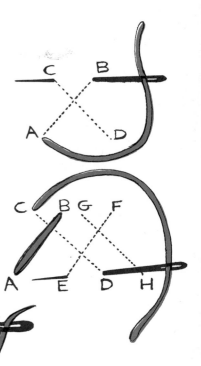

*Exquisitely worked Satin stitches make the flowers in this detail from an old Slovakian vest in the Brooklyn Museum.*

### The Split Stitch

This stitch is done in a manner similar to the Stem stitch on page 29. But now as you move backward on each stitch split the thread with your needle and pull through. This looks like a fine Chain stitch.

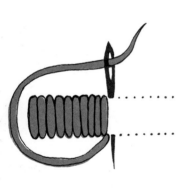

### The Satin Stitch

You have probably used this stitch instinctively. Since the beginning of embroidery the Satin stitch has been used to fill in areas. It looks very easy but actually it's quite tricky to make it look well, and have a clean neat edge. To get a firm neat line around the edge, outline the area first with the Split stitch and then, when doing the Satin stitch, insert the needle over the outside edge of the outline. Another way is to start in the center and work toward each end.

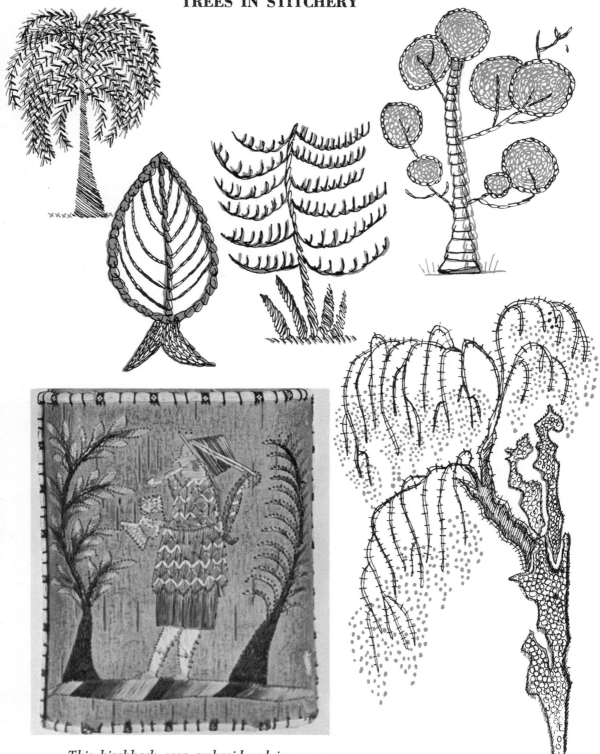

*This birchbark case embroidered in moose hair was made by Indians in Huron, Canada.* Museum of the American Indian, Heye Foundation.

## TAKE A STITCHERY WALK

So far, we have been talking about practicing stitches so you can learn to sew them. Now it is time to try a project. We want you to discover the different effects you can get with a stitch, to see how each stitch behaves for you, and to have the fun of making a stitchery of your own.

Plan a stitchery walk. It could be around a city block, up a mountainside, or down along the seashore.

Begin with a nice fat yarn for Couching and let this yarn become the path of your walk. When the path pleases you, fasten it down with pins. You'll find it easier to work by keeping it flat on a table. Be careful to leave at least a two-inch margin all around because you should turn back the edge when it's finished.

Now, test out different yarn colors by laying them on the background fabric to see where they look best. In working out your picture walk idea, it's helpful to cut out simple paper shapes and pin them down like a pattern. It gives you an idea of what the finished stitchery will be like.

This is the time to have your practice piece at hand, so that you can refer to it and see how your Flat stitches looked in thread. The Back stitch and the Stem stitch are both good for making the outlines of a house, or a horse, or for filling in a boat. The Cross stitch makes a good tile roof or a fence. The Fern stitch, naturally, looks like a little tree, and in the rows of a garden plot you can line up all the stitches you have learned.

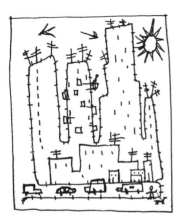

This is just one idea for a stitchery walk. We're sure you can invent a hundred others. What about a walk on the moon, or around a city at night, or along a coral reef under the sea? Let your imagination wander!

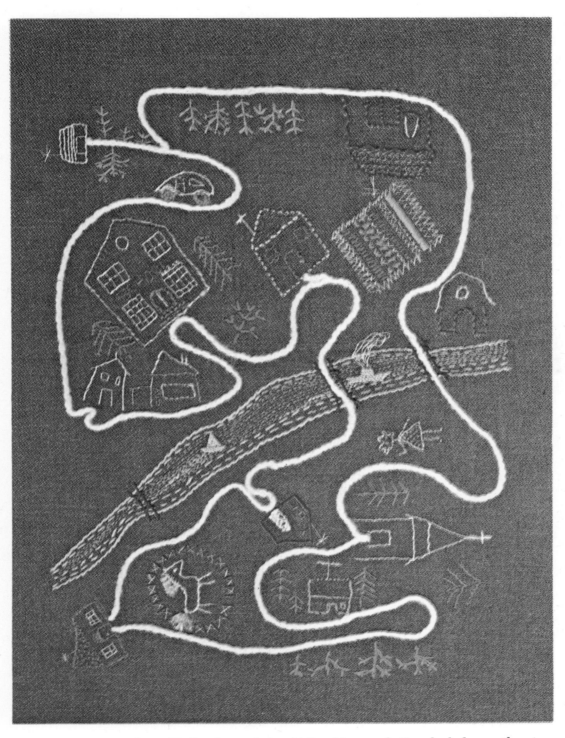

A Stitchery Walk: the path in thick white wool, Couched down; the river in Running stitches; the houses in Back stitches; the horse corral in Cross and Flat stitches; the garden—a little sampler of Flat stitches.

*Stick figures
in Flat stitches.*

Chapter Four

## NOW BECOME AN INVENTOR

You've learned the flat stitches. Now let's see what you can do to invent variations on these stitches.

Flat stitches like the Running stitch can move in any direction. They're perfect for little stick figures, but don't jump from head to foot—always move to the next stitch.

Now try *Threading* on a Running stitch. This second thread lies on the surface of the cloth, except at the beginning and end. Start at the right and come up just below the first Running stitch. Now slide the needle upward under the first Running stitch without going through the fabric. Then slide downward under the next Running stitch, and so on. This has the formal name of the Single Threaded Running stitch.

How would you do a Double Threaded Running stitch? Simply do the Single again, this time in reverse direction.

Threading has an even more interesting effect when used with the Back stitch. Try it!

Here's another one to experiment with. It's called the Whipped stitch. You go over and over a Running stitch or a Back stitch in the same way you Couched down a heavy thread, but here you simply slide under the stitches without going through the fabric.

38

How many ways can you Couch? Here are a few.

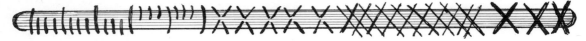

You can vary the Herringbone stitch by using with it a little flat tack-down stitch. Then we call it a Tacked Herringbone.

Or you can go over the cross and under the diagonal lines. This we call a Threaded or Interlaced Herringbone.

See how many more stitches or combinations you can invent. And keep a record of them on your sample piece of material.

## Holiday Decorations

For the project in this chapter we have chosen holiday decorations. We have used felt and Pellon for the background shapes. They are excellent for such decorations because they don't unravel, making it unnecessary to turn edges.

Felt comes in lovely bright colors and is sold by the yard in fabric departments. You can often find small squares in places like the ten-cent store. Pellon comes in different weights and is also sold by the yard. In upholstery departments you can get it in narrow bands, which is very convenient for small shapes. The medium or heavy weights of Pellon are best to use for these projects. You need a sharp-pointed needle and you should not try to pull a thick thread through this kind of material. Couch thick or uneven threads.

Pellon also comes with an iron-on backing. This is a very convenient way to easily line the backs of the decorations. Be sure to cut the lining larger than your decoration and trim it after it's been ironed on.

*A Valentine heart in Threaded Back stitch, Herringbone, Couching, Fern, and Cross stitches.*

*Embroidered Easter egg decorations of Pellon and felt were all worked with flat stitches. They are easy to make.*

These interlining fabrics are generally white, and they take color beautifully. You can use either a felt pen or ordinary wax crayons. With crayons, you must press down hard to get strong colors. When you're ready to remove the crayon wax from the surface, simply put a paper towel over it, press with a warm iron, and lift the paper towel up quickly. This also sets the color.

As to the shapes of the decorations, we suggest you begin with simple ones. Trace around a cup or cookie cutter. A piece of paper, folded in half before cutting, will give you a shape with identical sides when opened. Pin the paper pattern to the fabric and cut around it.

Once you've cut out the shape and colored it with the felt pen or crayon, decorate it with stitchery.

The threads will become color accents on the painted or crayoned design. For example, if you've used yellow crayon or ink, choose threads in orange, pink, and red. They are all in the same warm color family, and work well together. If you've used pale blue ink or crayon, then pick threads in green, violet, and a different blue. They also fit well together, since they are in the same cool color family. In another decoration you might experiment with a warm color against a cool color, or a dark against a light tone.

*Gay Christmas decorations like these give you a chance to be inventive with stitchery.*

*Drawing of embroidery on a Slovakian peasant shawl. Early 19th century.*

*Birds like these decorated Hungarian peasant costumes.*

*This bird in a tree was embroidered in Crewel work on a bedspread made in Boston in 1770. Metropolitan Museum of Art, Rogers Fund, 1922.*

*The fantastic bird on the left is drawn from a Cretan embroidery in* The Metropolitan Museum of Art. *The Slovakian bird, above, echoes its design but is much cruder.*

*Susan's stitchery Easter egg was decorated with a Chain-stitched bird.*

## Chapter Five

## LAZY DAISY, SEED, AND CHAIN

We now come to the Chain stitch, which has been used by embroiderers for thousands of years. It has been found on ancient fabrics made long, long ago in Egypt, in China, and in Peru. It has many variations.

### The Chain Stitch

This stitch moves from top to bottom, or toward yourself along an imaginary single line.

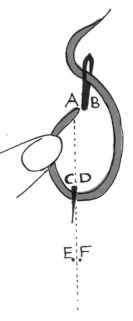

Come up at **A.** Hold the thread down with your thumb to form a loop. Put the needle back in at **B**—in the same hole as **A** or just next to it. Now come up below at **C**—inside the loop, and keep holding the thread down with your thumb or you'll lose the loop. Now put the needle in at **D,** still inside the loop.

And so on. When you get to the end of a line, finish it off by taking a tack-down stitch on the last loop. We really should call this one the Thumb stitch.

Try it in different ways. Make large chains with thick yarns in a loose and open manner; make others with a tighter, closed look. Do the same with thin thread.

The popularity of the Chain stitch shows how useful a stitch it is. It may be your favorite for drawing a fine elegant line, as well as for filling in delicate spots or large rugged areas. On this page you see details from a tablecloth made in present-day Iran. The colorful little figures are embroidered in cotton, using only the Chain stitch.

Young boys in India embroidered the rug shown on the opposite page. The carefree designs are worked in heavy wool and also use only the Chain stitch. These Namda rugs are very popular in America today. In India the word Namda simply means rug.

*The woman smoking a water pipe and the man leading his camel are figures embroidered all in Chain stitch on a present-day tablecloth made in Iran.*

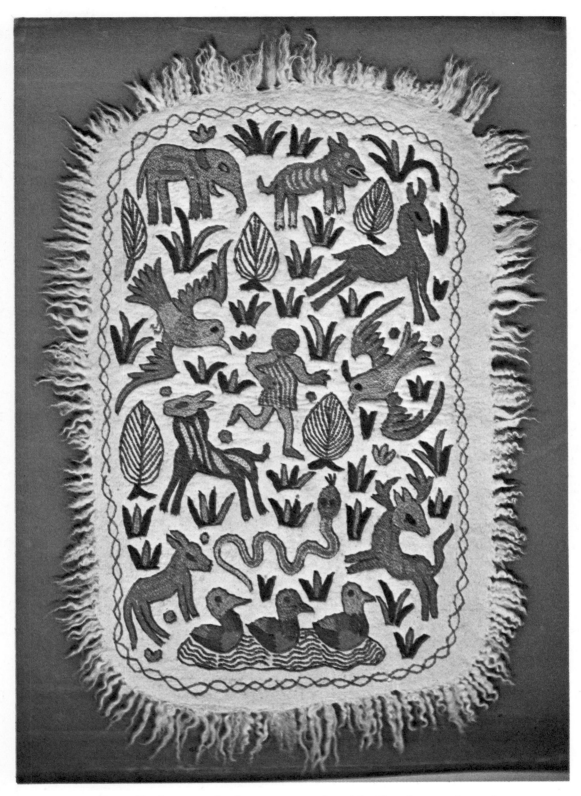

*Another all-Chain stitch decoration is this felt Namda rug from India. Animal figures—like the elephant and cobra—are typical motifs.*

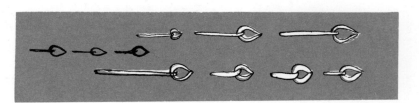

### The Detached Chain Stitch

This is also called Seed stitch and Powder stitch. Each link in the chain is separate. Make just one loop and tack it down. You can make the loops one after the other in a line, or you can scatter them so they look like seeds. You can vary the length of the tack-down stitch for different effects.

### The Lazy Daisy Stitch

These are Detached Chain stitches sewn in a circle to form flower petals. Start at the center, putting the tack-down stitch on the outside.

### Spoke Variation of the Lazy Daisy

Reverse the Detached Chain so that you start at the outside of the circle. Now the tack-down stitches will be in the center, and you can vary their length for different effects. Try these stitches with several different weights of thread.

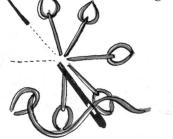

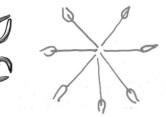

## The Open Chain Stitch

The plain Chain stitch moved toward you on an imaginary single line. The Open Chain stitch moves toward you on two imaginary lines, and you move back and forth from one side to the other. It makes a squared-off loop instead of the rounded one you got with the plain Chain.

Up at **A.** In at **B.**
Out at **C.** In again at **D.**

Don't forget the thumb hold, and keep the thread loose.

Try inventing some Chain stitches of your own. You'll get surprising results.

Try a line of Chain stitches. Do the Back stitch down the center.

Try Threaded Chains.

Try Open Chains overlapping.

And don't forget to try Couching down with Chains.

*Detached Chains make the flower shapes on the tote bag. On the clutch purse—Plain, Couched, and Threaded Chains. On the glass case—Open Chain.*

## CHAIN STITCH BAGS

The embroidered bags and the eyeglass case shown here were decorated with Chain stitches. We hope they will give you ideas for bags of your own design.

*The Clutch Purse.* The purse shown here is made of heavy linen and measures 8½×14 inches. To make one like it, first cut two pieces of fabric the same size—one for the bag and one for the lining. Since you embroider only the front flap, fold the fabric in three parts to determine the position of your embroidery. Be sure to allow enough margin for seams. After you have finished the embroidery, stitch the fabric and lining together, face to face, but leave the inside top edge open. Trim the edges down to at least ¼ inch, clip the corners, turn the bag right side out, and press. Now whip the open edge together neatly, fold, and sew up the sides of the purse.

*The Tote Bag.* Our tote bag was made of heavy canvas, decorated mainly with Detached Chains. To make one like it, cut two pieces of fabric, each 36×12 inches, one

THE DETACHED CHAIN

## EYEGLASS CASE

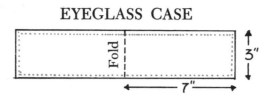

Fold

3"

7"

## CLUTCH PURSE

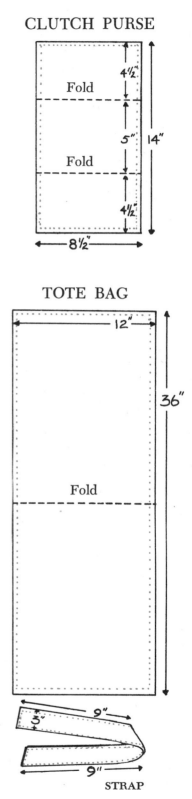

Fold

4½"

5"

14"

Fold

4½"

8½"

## TOTE BAG

12"

36"

Fold

3"

9"

9"

**STRAP**

for the bag and one for the lining. For the handle and its lining, cut two smaller pieces, 18×3 inches.

Plan the design to fit the size and shape of the bag. A good way to begin is to cut different-sized circles out of paper, using cups, cans, jar tops, coins, etc., for size. Now baste a margin line for the design area. Within this area arrange your paper circles, moving them around until the design pleases you. Keep in mind that the open spaces between the circles are important to the design. Now pin the paper circles in place and draw a line around them with chalk or baste around them. You are now ready to embroider.

The Detached Chain stitches, in all their variations, lend themselves perfectly to circle designs. Just as you varied the sizes of the circles, so you can vary the thickness and texture of the threads, as well as the colors. You might begin by stitching one circle with a Lazy Daisy, starting at the center. In the next circle you might stitch a line of plain Chain on the outside and work toward the center with long-stemmed Detached Chains. There are many possibilities.

When you've finished embroidering, sew the bag and lining together on the reverse side, but leave the top and bottom open. Do the same with the strap. Now trim the seams and turn right sides out. Fold the bag in two and insert the strap between bag and lining, having turned in the open top edges. Sew across the top of the bag. This will finish off the edges and lock the strap into position. Now sew up the sides.

*The Eyeglass Case.* You make this just as you did the tote bag, omitting the strap. The small rectangular shape is ideal for stitching with Open Chain.

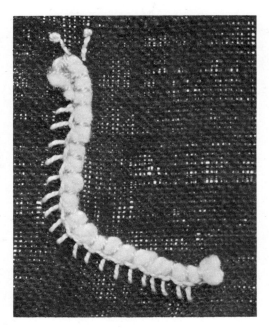

A *Buttonhole stitch caterpillar,
a part of a wall hanging
made by 11-year-old Andy.*

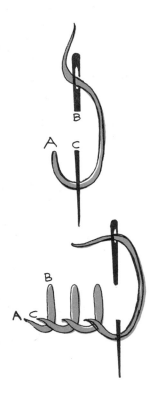

Chapter Six

## THE LOOPED LION AND CRETAN CAT

In this chapter you will learn some of the stitches in the group made up of Looped stitches. They are part of a very large family. The grandmother of them all is the Buttonhole stitch. And there are many cousins, aunts, and uncles, some of them with very exotic names.

Present-day embroiderers are changing the traditional ways of working these stitches, changing both the sizes and the ways of combining them, in order to make them less formal than they were in the past.

### Buttonhole or Blanket Stitch

This stitch was used for edging blankets. Variations of it are used for making buttonholes. Here we use it, not to edge the cloth, but as allover decoration.

You move from left to right on the fabric. Come up at **A.** Hold the thread with the left thumb in the same way you did for the Chain stitch. With the needle pointing straight toward yourself, go down at **B** and come up at **C,** with the needle on top of the thread.

## Buttonhole Variation

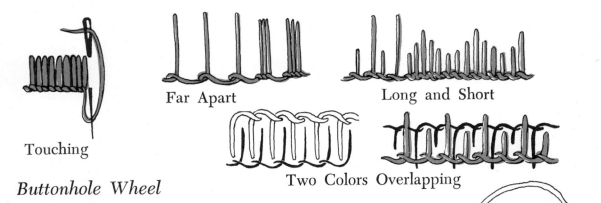

Touching

Far Apart

Long and Short

Two Colors Overlapping

### Buttonhole Wheel

You start on the outside of the circle. **B** is in the center. The top of each stitch can be in the same central hole, or can form an inner circle.

### Buttonhole Filling

Start as usual at the left but stop at the end of the first line. Change the position of your thread by throwing it over to the left and holding it down with your thumb in the same manner as before, and work the Buttonhole stitch to the end of the second line. Now throw the thread back to the right for the third line. The first stitch of each line is squared off when the next row comes back or on the last row a little tack-down stitch can be added.

### Detached Buttonhole

The Buttonhole stitch is now separated from the background material. A heading is needed to begin on, either a couple of straight stitches or a row of Chain stitches. The mechanics or movements are just the same as when you did the plain Buttonhole stitch but the effect is very different. Instead of piercing the material each time, the needle goes through just the previous row of stitches.

Be sure to try Couching with the Buttonhole stitch.

*The Buttonhole-stitch lion. By using different thicknesses of yarn, as well as different sizes of stitch, you get varied effects with the versatile Buttonhole.*

## Closed Buttonhole Stitch

This stitch reminds one of a tepee. It's trickier to make than the Plain Buttonhole. The execution is the same but the direction is different.

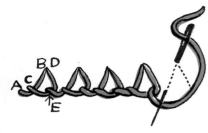

Begin the same way. Then, instead of pointing the needle straight up and down for the stitch **B–C,** move backward on a diagonal. The second stitch uses the same hole at the top and moves forward on the diagonal. Leave the thread slack and reach ahead for **E.** **B–D** form the top of a triangle.

## Crossed Buttonhole Stitch

This stitch looks even more like a tepee. It is very similar to the Closed Buttonhole. When reaching for point **D**, cross over and go down in front of **B**.

Try this stitch adding a tack-down stitch, as you did with the Herringbone.

*The lordly cat is all Feather and Cretan*
*stitch but the little white mouse is all Buttonhole.*

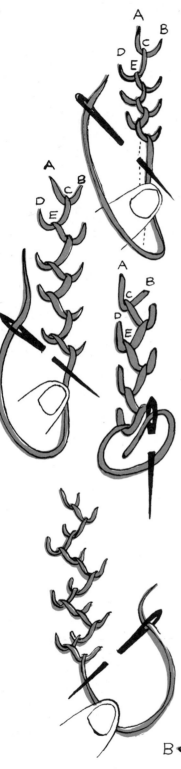

### Feather Stitch

Feather is a lovely stitch. It has a soft, sweet look to it and is quite naturally a favorite for babies' clothes. Yet variations can be bold and modern.

You start at the top and work toward yourself.

Come up at **A.**

With left thumb holding thread, go down at **B.**
Come up at **C,** straight down under **A.**
Throw thread to the left.
Again holding thread with thumb, put needle in at **D,** an equal distance down as at **B,** but on left side. Come up at **E.** Throw thread to right.
Alternate side to side each time.

Now work the Feather so that **B–C** is a small diagonal stitch. **C** will not be under **A;** nor will **E.** This gives the Feather a slightly different look.

Make the Feather again, with **B–C** coming straight toward you. It has a different look again.

### Double Feather Stitch

You do just what the name implies. Take two Feather stitches on each side.

### Closed Feather Stitch

This stitch begins in a different way from Feather.
**B** must be slightly higher than **A.**
**C** must be directly under **B.** Throw thread to left.
**D** goes in immediately under **A** so the thread touches and gives this stitch its name.
**E** must be directly under **D.**
This stitch makes a good border. With a fairly thick wool yarn it can have a bold, heavy look.

## Cretan Stitch

This stitch, which was once so popular on the island of Crete, is again a favorite with modern stitchers. It looks very complicated but it really isn't and you will soon see that it has a rhythm all its own. It will sweep you along as though you were riding into shore on a wave. Cretan is really a widened, flattened-out Feather stitch. In Feather, the stitch toward the center is taken on a diagonal line. In Cretan, this same stitch is more on a horizontal line.

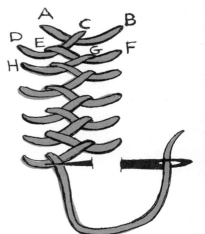

To start, come up at **A,** and with the thread on the right, take a small stitch (**B–C**) toward the center, on a horizontal line. Throw thread to the left.
Take a small stitch (**D–E**) toward the center. Throw thread to the right and continue.

Try it a second time, and make these same stitches move almost all the way to the center. Cretan stitch changes with the slant of your needle and the size of your stitch. If you have been using a thin thread, try it with a thick one and you will see that the Cretan stitch will change again.

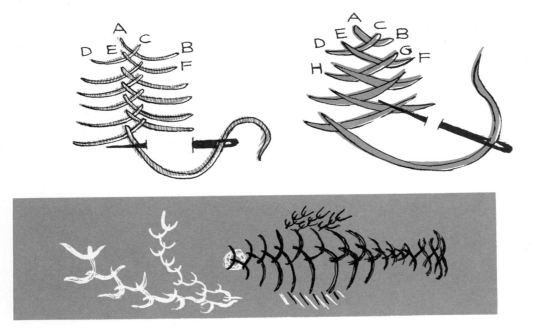

*Embroidery from Crete, done in the Cretan stitch.* Metropolitan Museum of Art, bequest of Richard B. Seager.

The Cretan stitch can be worked closely, as in the embroidery from Crete shown here. This way it has a solid, filled-in effect. It can also be more spread out, as you see it in the birds on a skirt from Ecuador. You can get very freewheeling designs with Cretan. It's a most versatile stitch.

## A PILLOW ZOO

A pillow for your bed should be gay and colorful. We've made a few to start you off. The lion was stitched on a heavy cotton upholstery cloth. The bird is on a wool tweed. The cat and mouse are on velveteen. The cat stalking the bird is on linen. If you decide to stitch an animal design, choose an animal whose shape fits the kind of pillow you want. Remember to baste at least a three-inch margin all around. Look for strong, interesting fabrics as background and don't make your stitches too large or too loose or they will catch on buttons. If they do get too large, use tackdown or Couching stitches to hold them in place.

If you examine the photographs carefully you will see why we called this chapter "The Looped Lion and Cretan Cat."

*A bolder use of the Cretan stitch in the detail of a skirt from Ecuador.* Costume Institute, Metropolitan Museum of Art, gift of Caroline Schnurer.

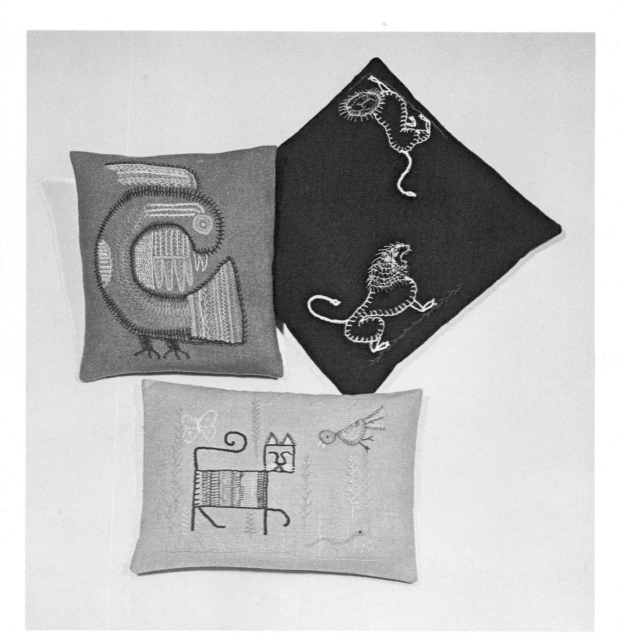

*A collection of animal pillows, all embroidered
in Looped stitches—Cretan, Feather, and Buttonhole.*

# INSECTS IN STITCHERY

*Drawn from 19th-century German samplers.* Metropolitan Museum of Art, bequest of Mrs. Lathrop Colgate Harper.

*Insects were popular embroidery motifs in most countries. This delightful grasshopper at the spinning wheel decorated a 19th-century card case.*

*Some of the world's most elegant embroidery is found on French costumes. Detail from an 18th-century white satin waistcoat.* Brooklyn Museum.

*This little Chain-stitch mouse was made by 10-year-old Susan.*

*The deer design, shown here, was much used in Hungary.*

*A hunter and his dogs. Detail from a Czechoslovakian embroidered bed curtain. Note use of outlining stitch.*

*Black woolen chair-cushion covers like this one, embroidered in bright colors, were popular in 18th-century Sweden. Brooklyn Museum collection.*

*A Slovakian child's bonnet with embroidered French knots on white linen.* Brooklyn Museum.

## Chapter Seven

# A KNOTTY PROBLEM

This is a knotty problem which is easily solved. The three knot stitches in this chapter only *look* difficult, but are really quite simple. Ordinarily, you would use knots in combination with other stitches, as the French knots in the flower centers on the opposite page. However, the best way to learn each stitch is to keep at it until you have explored all its possibilities.

### The French Knot

A French knot is a very tiny stitch and you would not generally use it all by itself. Yet, in the Slovakian bonnet shown above, someone with infinite patience did use minute white French knots for the entire design.

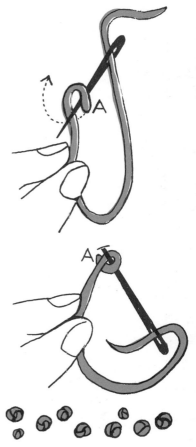

With a single thread in your needle, come up at **A.**
Hold the thread between left thumb and index finger.
Point the needle left, just above **A.**
Wind the thread up and over the needle once.
Go down immediately above **A.**

Try this with a double thread in your needle.

To get larger knots, use more strands of thread, rather than winding over and over. This only builds the knot higher and makes it wobbly.

French knots can be packed tightly, or done in a line, or spread out.

*A linen napkin, folded in half, can be made into an attractive head kerchief with embroidery. This one uses only Knot stitches.*

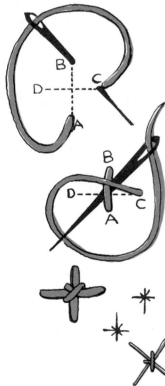

## Four-legged Knot Stitch

This is a stitch which can also be either lined up or scattered like stars in a night sky.

Come up at **A.** Go down at **B,** directly above.
Come up at **C** and stop.
Lay thread toward the left, across center of **A–B.** The needle slides diagonally under the center, where the threads cross, but *not* through the fabric. The point of the needle goes on top of the thread held by your left thumb. Now pull the thread through, helping the knot in the center to fall into place.
To finish, go down at **D.**
If the knot in the center looks too skimpy, you can repeat the knot phase before going down at **D.**

## Coral Stitch

This stitch gives you a nice bumpy, jagged line.
Work from right to left. Come up at **A.**
Hold thread straight to left with your thumb.
Go down at **B,** immediately above thread.
Come up at **C,** immediately below thread.
Point of needle should be on top of thread you are
holding with your thumb. Hold until you pull up knot.
To finish, go down right next to the last knot.

## Zigzag Coral

A variation of the Coral is the *Zigzag Coral.* Follow the
same instructions as for the Coral but make one knot
up, and one knot down, in a zigzag line.

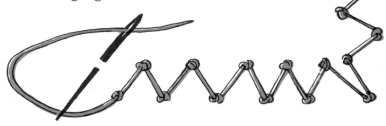

## Detached Coral

You can do with the Coral what you did with the
Chain. Besides stitching it in a continuous line, you
can detach it. After each knot, anchor it immediately
below the knot or near the stem. This is a very effective
stitch for circles or flowers.

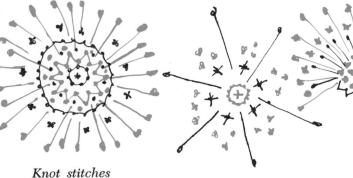

*Knot stitches
in different
combinations
make interesting
flower patterns.*

*A variety of Knot stitches were used to decorate these embroidered accessories—headbands, belts, a purse.*

## HEADBANDS AND BELTS

For these small knot stitches we have chosen small projects of headbands, belts, and a kerchief. They are very popular. Embroider one for yourself and then make some as gifts for your friends.

A stretch headband is a soft, easy background for stitching and allows you to use a variety of threads. Grosgrain and velvet ribbons are also good and come in beautiful colors. Begin by cutting a length, leaving a two-inch space for the back of your head so that you can add either a strip of flat elastic tape or two elastic threads. Giant rickrack tape, mounted on ribbon, makes a striking belt. For accents you might use heavy, rugged Knot stitches.

Carpet binding sounds unglamorous for a headband but it works very well. It comes in a variety of soft colors and is a very good background for embroidery. A self-lining of the same binding, or of a wider grosgrain ribbon, is suitable. Carpet binding comes in two widths. Use the narrow for a headband, the wide for a belt.

Stretch belting is sold by the yard, so you can make your own belt by simply attaching a cinch buckle. Heavy linen, embroidered and folded over, with a fringe added to the ends, makes a handsome sash.

Hand-embroidered accessories like these will give your outfits a very individual touch.

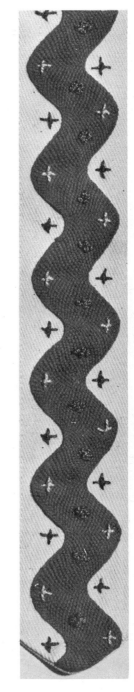

*A belt of narrow carpet binding, trimmed with giant rickrack and a few Cross-legged Knot stitches.*

*"Ellen Childe her Booke—1653" is inscribed
on this Bible. The embroidered binding is typical
of English work at this time. Morgan Library.*

*Drawing of detail
in Ellen Childe's
elaborate cover,
shown above.*

## Chapter Eight

## GIFTS FOR A QUEEN

In 1544, when Queen Elizabeth I was eleven years old, she copied out by hand a volume called *The Mirror or Glasse of the Synneful Soule*—a frightening title. It must have been an important book to her because she also embroidered for it a velvet cover. This copy still exists in the Bodleian Library at Oxford, England.

In the sixteenth and seventeenth centuries it was very fashionable to embroider an elaborate book cover with metallic and silver threads, often embellished with jewels.

The book cover shown here was made in 1652 by a young Englishwoman named Ellen Childe.

*Drawing shows how to fold and make a book cover out of nonwoven material like Pellon.*

Today we do not live in so elegant an age, but a "queenly" book cover still makes a wonderful gift. Pellon is perfect for such a project: it does not unravel, and can easily be folded and stitched.

Again, this will be a time to experiment with color freely. You can use either crayons or felt pens or the brilliantly colored waterproof drawing inks which are sold in stationery stores. The inks can be painted on Pellon with a brush. They will give you a bright splashy effect and you can overpaint one color on another to give you a third color.

Try a small book cover at first, perhaps a notebook or a diary. Cut a piece of medium- or heavyweight Pellon, at least two inches bigger than the height of the book, and wide enough so you will be able to make deep pockets on each side. Make a three-quarter-inch fold both at top and bottom. This will still leave you a quarter-inch extension above and below and you will need this later when you come to stitch the edges. Now center the book and fold the sides.

*A personal cover for a personal book, made with Pellon, crayons, and stitchery.*

After you have made your decoration in color and stitchery, finish off the edges with a Whipped or Buttonhole stitch, or whatever you think will be attractive.

*Embroidered photograph album cover of Pellon, made by a young lady who stitches better than she spells.*

In making the decoration, you will be faced with a few limitations because heavy needles and threads are difficult to pull through Pellon, even with the help of a thimble. But the solution is simple. Heavy threads can be Couched on with the same color in mercerized cotton thread, or one to two strands of embroidery floss. Bright touches can be added later with sequins or small beads.

Who wouldn't want to receive a personal book cover like this? It might become a family heirloom.

*Two small notebook covers, one with inks and colored stitchery on white Pellon, the other with only white stitches on black Pellon.*

*Make your own Pellon cards.*

## Holiday Card

Make your own card to go with your gift. Add the stitchery as the last part of your design and be sure to do some of the stitches with plain ordinary mercerized cottons or thin strands of embroidery floss. If you cut your card double the finished size you can fold it in half and you have a lining ready to stitch down and cover your knots.

## Bookmark

A handmade bookmark is an ideal small remembrance all by itself, and can be made with Pellon or carpet binding fringed on each end.

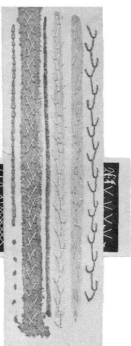

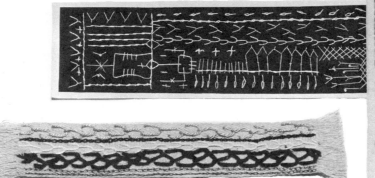

*Embroidered bookmarks are small but thoughtful gifts.*

*Flat stones, driftwood, a skate's egg case, shells, a tiny horseshoe crab—these and many other beachcombings can be stitched down with Herringbone, Buttonhole, or flat stitches with Knots.*

## Chapter Nine

## STICKS AND STONES

It may surprise you to know that sticks and stones and many other unexpected things can be very useful in stitchery.

You have seen how King Powhatan's cloak (page 9) was decorated with cowrie shells and how the ancient Peruvian shirt (page 9) was stitched with bird feathers. The natives of East India embroidered with shining beetle wings and mirrorlike pieces of mica which they Buttonhole-stitched onto their clothing.

Now look at this feather apron of the Jivaro Indians from the jungles of South America. Sewn onto it are yellow and orange feathers together with red seeds and small broken pieces of bird bone. If you examine it closely you will also see the whole skin of a brightly colored bird.

Many of our modern weavers and stitchers do very much the same sort of thing. For instance, they will often use dried grasses and reeds or driftwood in making a wall hanging. Of course, this type of stitchery is not practical for pillows or for clothing.

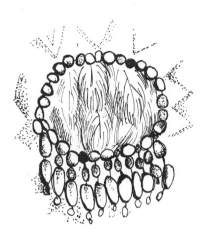

*It's not a mask but a man's apron, stitched with feathers, seeds, and bird bones by the Jivaro Indians of Ecuador. Above is a detail drawing.*
Museum of the American Indian, New York.

Begin to look around you and you will see the endless variety of things you might use.

The seashore is a treasure-trove to an embroiderer with an imaginative eye. Gather bits of broken shells, especially the ones with holes which the sea worms have so conveniently bored for you. The tiny pebbles and fragments of colored glass, polished by the sea, can be the jewel-like accents on your embroidery. Certain dried seaweeds form interesting shapes. And don't overlook bleached fishbones with their intricate designs, lobster claws, dainty crab shells, and the dried black egg cases of the skate.

Late summer is the time to look for the lovely shining wings of a dead dragonfly or those marvelous empty skins left behind by the beetle and the cicada.

In early autumn, when the grasses are drying in the fields, you can collect golden stalks. But first run your fingers up the seed head to see which are usable. Some fall apart, but others will hold together a long time. Seed pods are also good starting points for a nature stitchery. We recommend the milkweed pod, the bittersweet, and the silver honesty.

If you live in the city, there is no need to be frustrated. Today, florist shops and garden centers have large selections of dried flowers and pods.

The winter is also a good time to hunt in the park or the woods for treasures you can use in stitchery. Pieces of bark are lying all about, waiting to add pattern to your design. It would be interesting to collect twigs, each with its distinctive winter bud. And in moist places you will often find the sensitive fern, with its tough stalk rising above the winter snow.

When you have a collection for your nature stitchery, it is time to think of how you will use it. If you are making a wall hanging, you will need a strong background fabric. A heavy linen or canvas works very well. Burlap is also good if your objects are not too heavy. It would not be right to stitch pebbles, for instance, to a thin, weak fabric. As you sew, hold up your hanging from time to time and make sure the weight is not too great for the background fabric.

*Cross stitch, Open Chain, Feather, and Couching—for attaching plants.*

This type of embroidery needs to be done with a bold and inventive style. After some practice your stitches will adapt themselves to the nature of the objects with which you are working. Flat stitches are indispensable for fastening down pebbles and shells. The Open Chain and Feather stitches are good for attaching a branch or a twig, while the fragile grasses can be gently Whipped in place. For enclosing slippery fragments, try a basket arrangement of Herringbone stitches.

*This stitchery of a seashore walk was made with beachcombings. The Feather and Cretan stitches form the seaweed.*

The golden tones of corn and wheat are accented with brown stitchery. Note how well the Feather and Herringbone stitches hold down the stems.

As you work out your design and plan where your objects will go, it's a good idea to make a rough sketch on paper. Then you can lay aside those objects which are fragile or bulky and work first on your basic stitchery design. Later add your sticks and stones as you would add icing to a cake.

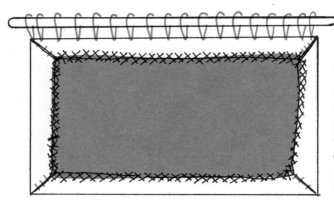

*Three ways to finish the back of a hanging. LEFT: By stitching on a backing of fabric. BELOW: By overlapping on a wood panel and lacing with string. BOTTOM: By stapling to the back of a canvas stretcher.*

A nature hanging is sometimes heavy, and often fragile, so it needs a firm backing or mounting. One way to do this is to turn the edges of the hanging and Whip a heavy fabric to the back. If it seems to be needed, you might even place a piece of cardboard in between, as a stiffener. To hang it, you can slide a wooden dowel or a metal curtain rod through an opening at the top, or you can Whip the rod directly to the top of the hanging with a strong thread.

Another method of mounting is to stretch the hanging over a thin board made of Masonite or quarter-inch plywood. Lace the lap-overs at the back with a strong thread from side to side and from top to bottom, always beginning in the middle of each side and working out to the edges. This method can be used only if you have left a wide margin all around the hanging and if the fabric is strong enough to be pulled taut.

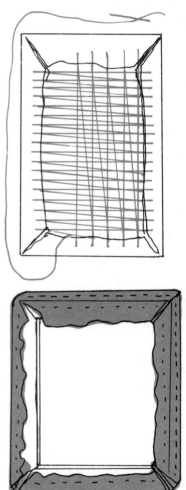

A large hanging would be too heavy mounted on a solid board and is better stapled to the stretchers made for artists to stretch canvas, which you buy in an art supply store. Double-faced tape can also be used for hanging a piece and is particularly useful where no margin of fabric was left for turning.

If you are in school, a hanging could be a project in botany or biology. A group could work together on a stitchery mural using grasses, twigs, and seed heads.

These nature hangings will give you an idea of some of the possibilities of combining nature's materials with stitchery.

*A portrait banner in machine stitchery by Norman LaLiberté.*

*An ancient portrait in stitchery, made over 1200 years ago in Coptic Egypt.* Courtesy of The Brooklyn Museum.

## Chapter Ten

## STITCHERY PORTRAITS AND DOLLS

### PORTRAITS

On these pages are two stitchery portraits. The one above was made over twelve hundred years ago in Egypt. The one on the left was made in 1964 in New York. Strange what a similarity there is in these two faces, which are so far apart in time, distance, and technique. The Egyptian fragment was made by hand with tiny stitches and the little girl gazes out at you from the remoteness of a culture long past. The "Portrait of a Lady" by Norman LaLiberté was made with an imaginative use of fabric appliqué and was stitched by machine.

There are as many different ways to make a portrait in stitches as there are people to stitch them. You, too, can make a stitchery portrait.

*Andy's self-portrait—age 10.*

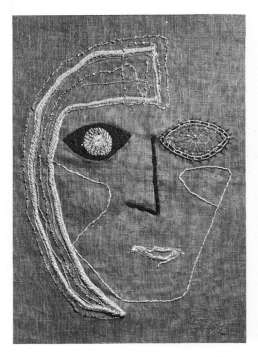

*Lee's stitchery portrait on red linen.*
*Interesting eye detail is shown on the left.*

*Heavy yarns for the hair, satin, Pellon, and net for the flowers, stitchery for details like the eye— portrait with flowered hat.*

Andy was only ten when she made this portrait of herself with her new ski poles. Since she had only just begun to learn embroidery she knew only a few flat stitches, but she made good use of them. We think it was a fine idea to make a great, fat braid of heavy wool, and to stitch loose threads for bangs.

The other portrait on the opposite page was made by Lee on red linen using mostly pink and purple yarns. You can see that what interested her most was the large outline of the face, the intensity of the eyes, and the rhythmic lines of the hair, which she Couched down with orange yarns.

The portrait with a flowered hat is yet another approach. Here appliquéd cutouts give great variety, and the heavy wool yarn, Couched down, makes an interesting texture for the hair.

*Paper cutouts of the heads will help you form
the design of your family portrait in stitchery.*

And why not a *family* portrait?
Work out your plans first by cutting the figure shapes
out of paper. This gives you the chance to experiment
in arranging the faces so that some look forward and
some are in profile. It is easy to place one person behind
another by shifting the paper forms. Change them
around until the arrangement satisfies you.

Place these paper patterns on your background material and then trace around them with chalk to give
yourself guidelines. Pick up one figure at a time and
duplicate it by cutting it out of fabric. Features can be

*The finished family portrait—appliquéd fabrics for the large areas, crayoned Pellon for faces and hands, stitchery for the details. The smoke is a Couched-down yarn.*

embroidered before a face is sewn to the background. Clothing can be made quickly and colorfully by using scraps of printed fabrics and tweeds with little or no embroidery and then appliquéd down.

Let your imagination run wild—add a bit of lace, a tie, buttons or jewelry, your dog's old license tag, or a bell on the cat.

This will not be a quick project. It will take lots of planning. You will change your plans many times, but that is always part of working out an idea.

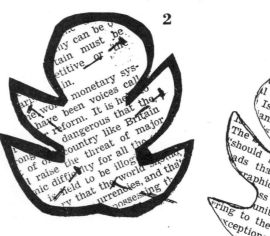

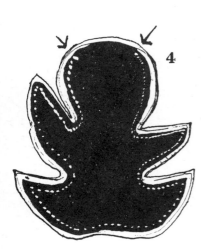

## Dolls

Dolls are more than just toys. They can be another kind of portrait. They can be an amusing, colorful accent on your bed. They can illustrate with embroidery the decorative traditions of a country. If you look at a book on folk art in your local library you will see that each nation has its own distinctive type of doll. We have taken five very different dolls from five different cultures to use as inspiration for our modern dolls.

A doll can easily be made from two identical pieces, front and back, put together like a sandwich. First draw on paper a very simple shape the exact size of your doll. This will be your pattern. When you use this paper pattern to cut fabric, be sure to leave more than a half-inch all around for seam allowance.

Next, do your embroidery on one of the pieces of fabric. Then turn them on the reverse side and sew around, except for an opening at the top or the bottom so you can put in your stuffing. Finally, trim the edges down to a quarter-inch, clip any corners or curves, and turn the doll right side out.

Use cotton wadding or shredded foam for stuffing, being sure to push it into the corners with a pencil. If you want the doll to stand up, stuff it tightly and weight it with a stone at the bottom. When the doll is stuffed, Whip the opening together.

To Make a Rag Doll

**1.** *Cut out paper pattern.*

**2.** *Pin pattern to fabric.*

**3.** *Front side embroidered.*

**4.** *Front and back sections sewn together on reverse side. Opening (between arrows) is for stuffing.*

To Make a Foam-filled Doll

**1.** *Cut horse shape out of foam.*
**2.** *Sew together by machine two horse shapes in jersey. Leave opening for stuffing. Trim edges close.* **3.** *Decorate, then insert foam and sew up opening.*

A very different way to make a doll is to cut the pattern from a flat piece of foam rubber. It can be any thickness you like. Make a covering of fabric for the foam doll shape, being careful to cut the fabric extra large so that it will cover the sides of the foam, as well as give you enough extra for the seams.

As you did with the other type doll, sew the front and back of the doll together—but—only sew as indicated in the sketch or you will not be able to insert the foam doll. This opening will be big enough for your hand to fit, so that you can now easily decorate the doll with embroidery. Then close the opening by Whipping it together. Wool jersey or stretch fabrics are particularly good for making a doll by this method.

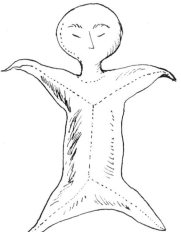

*The tall purple stitchery doll and the orange rag doll with the pink hair were inspired by the dolls from other lands drawn at the left. The top one is an ancient Egyptian painted wooden doll; the other is Japanese.*

The ancient Egyptian doll was made from a flat piece of wood, intricately painted, with a wild mop of woolly hair. The modern doll derived from it also has wild and woolly hair, but the designs are stitched instead of painted.

The cloth doll from Japan was made with a fine, simple shape and delicately stitched eyebrows. This version follows the seam lines with decorative stitchery and has a red yarn coiffure.

*The foam-filled jersey doll in the picture was patterned*
*on the painted wooden horse from Sweden, drawn above.*
*The other was based on the Indian Kachina doll,*
*also made of painted wood and drawn here at the right.*

Painted Swedish wooden horses have an embroidered
look and show Scandinavian folk designs. Our horse
was cut out of foam rubber and covered with orange
jersey.

*Kachina* dolls were made by Pueblo Indians. The
*Kachina* was the Great Spirit, who brought rain for
their crops and good health to their people. The
*Kachina* doll that we used is Hahai-Wügti, the Mother
of all the *Kachinas*.

## Chapter Eleven

## STITCHERY BANNERS

In medieval times embroidered banners were both decorative and important. Every fiefdom had its own emblem in its own special colors, and when armies marched into battle you could tell from their banners which castle they came from, and to which lord they pledged allegiance. The Crusaders carried them at the head of their lines, for banners were also used to show religious beliefs. At the medieval jousting tournaments, the field was gay with pennants flying from the spectators' balconies, while the embroidered standards of the knights and their companies ranged below in brilliant splashes of color.

Wedding banners were a custom, long ago, in some countries of central Europe. Every young girl hoped to have a special embroidered wedding banner in her trousseau. Often it showed the wedding procession on horseback with musicians, best man, bridesmaids, and the bride riding in a carriage.

The Czechoslovakian wedding banner pictured here was stitched in 1848. It is designed like a comic strip. First we see the courting couple, then the bride proudly exhibiting her trousseau of linens piled high on the bed. Next we see her rocking the cradle while the new father puffs his pipe in contentment. And then, in the last scene, we see the devoted husband bringing her a gift as she sits at her spinning wheel.

In later years, when village girls no longer spent so much of their time on embroidery, these beautiful wedding banners became rare, but lost none of their importance in the life of the village. The local church usually owned such a banner and would loan it to the bride for her wedding day.

*Embroidered wedding banners from Czechoslovakia often had designs like those sketched here. Source:* Textile Folk Art *by A. Vaclavik and J. Orel, Spring Books, London.*

*A machine-stitched banner made completely of Pellon and colored with oil crayons. Designed by Anita Askild.*

*A 4–H banner for the county fair. Fabric shapes were machine-stitched to felt; zigzag stitching for letters.*

*Black and white fake fur fabrics for the sheep, machine-stitched on a pink felt banner. The lettering is heavy wool yarn, basted down and stitched by machine.*

Banners are usually very large and it would take too long to stitch them by hand. The modern sewing machine is therefore a real boon to the banner maker. Pieces of fabric are appliquéd to a background in a jiffy, and you can use a straight Running stitch or a Zigzag stitch which completely covers the raveling edges. Zigzag machine stitching can be done in many varieties of stitch and width. It is a very effective way of writing your message in stitches.

Sometimes little pieces of fabric will be used more effectively if not completely attached. Notice the feathers on the rooster, or some of the flowers on the flower banner. Banners and posters are made to attract attention, so they should be simple in design. Be careful not to make them too complicated. Plan for a dramatic effect, use bold colors, and be sure the lettering is large and easy to read. You will be pleased that you became a collector of scraps of all kinds. Machine

*The members of the 4–H Dog Club were intent on telling the truth about their pets in this all-felt banner.*

stitching does not limit you to the use of thin threads, because here, too, you Couch down the heavy yarns, using any of the machine stitches. The stiffening fabrics, such as Pellon, are very well suited to banners or posters. Parts of your design can be cut from pieces of Pellon or transparent fabrics and colored with felt pens or inks and then machine stitched to a Pellon background. Before you begin to sew, pin and then baste all the parts of your design.

Banners are on their way to becoming as popular today as they were in the Middle Ages. Be original and stitch up a banner for your club!

Do you belong to the Girl Scouts? Think of all the events for which you could create a special banner! You can begin by making one to carry at the head of your troop when it next marches in a parade.

Are you a member of a 4–H Club? Think of all the ways you could use embroidered banners and pennants at your next county fair.

Do you belong to a young people's church group? Consider embroidering a banner for your church or temple.

Banners would make very dramatic posters! A flower banner would be a delightful surprise for your next spring party or flower show.

Most families have special ways of celebrating holidays or anniversaries, and a banner stitched by you for such a special occasion would be treasured by the whole family. What about a birthday banner for everyone in your family?

*Banner for a horse club made with printed cottons and letters cut out of white felt—all machine-stitched on purple felt.*

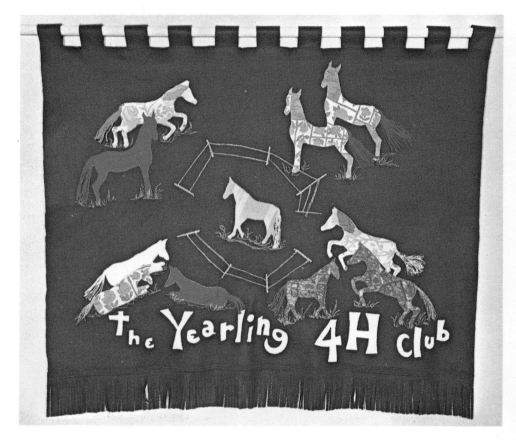

*The elephant never forgets, it is said,*
*and here is a sampler in the form of an elephant*
*pillow, using all the stitches described in*
*this book. How many can you identify?*

## Chapter Twelve

## SAMPLERS TWO

A sampler is a traditional piece of embroidery. It was not intended as a practice piece for learning stitches but was always a final record to show how skillfully a girl could do her stitches and how she could present them in an attractive design.

By now you have mastered many stitches and you have had the experience of using your imagination as you created your own projects. So for a final project in our book we think it only fitting to suggest a sampler—but a new and different kind of sampler. Instead of the formal sampler, which was framed and hung on the wall, our elephant and zebra samplers sit on the bed. They are a gay record of all the stitches in this book.

*The zebra pillow is also a sampler, using*
*many types of white yarn and thread to record*
*a variety of stitches on black wool.*

Embroidery is always changing, as you have seen from the many pictures in this book. Elizabeth Terry, who made the sampler on page 21, would have been very surprised to see these animals as samplers. She would have been amused at our holiday decorations, astounded by our banners, and she would never have thought of picking up shells from the beach or cornstalks from the field to combine with her yarns in making a hanging.

Nor could we have expected her to. She lived 136 years ago and the world was very different then. But people and customs change and embroidery has changed with them.

This book is meant to be used not for tedious tasks but for great pleasures. We hope it will open up for you the exciting world of stitchery.

# INDEX OF STITCHES

## About the Authors . . .

Winifred Lubell and Irene Miller are, individually and as a team, an incredible blending of imagination, skill, enthusiasm, and creative talents.

Co-author Winifred Lubell has illustrated twenty books for young readers, among them one written by herself and five written by her husband, Cecil. Mrs. Lubell studied art at the Art Students League in New York, and the Phillips Gallery School in Washington, D.C. When not at her drawing board, she gives "chalk talks" to youngsters in schools, creating wonderful drawings of birds, insects, flowers—anything her audience requests. She is the mother of two sons.

Irene Miller is a weaver and teacher of stitchery with a background in the teaching of art history and crafts to both children and adults. She is the mother of four, grandmother of one, and is active in 4-H and conservation work.

This energetic team enjoyed the year they spent on THE STITCHERY BOOK, researching, writing, gathering photographs, drawing, designing, making stitchery pieces—not to mention the time spent protecting the fruits of their labors from the Lubell cats and the Miller puppy (pictured below).